S⟨...⟩E

THE C⟨...⟩AITS

Susie Brooks

Published in paperback in 2017 by Wayland

Copyright © Wayland, 2017

All rights reserved.
ISBN: 978 1 5263 0025 6
10 9 8 7 6 5 4 3 2 1

Printed in China

Wayland
An imprint of
Hachette Children's Group
Part of Hodder & Stoughton
Carmelite House
50 Victoria Embankment
London EC4Y 0DZ

An Hachette UK Company
www.hachette.co.uk
www.hachettechildrens.co.uk

Editor: Elizabeth Brent
Designer: Lisa Peacock

The website addresses (URLs) and QR codes included in this book were valid at the time of going to press. However, it is possible that contents or addresses may have changed since the publication of this book. No responsibility for any such changes can be accepted by either the author or the Publisher.

Picture acknowledgements:
Cover: (top) The Art Archive/National Gallery London/Eileen Tweedy, (bottom middle) The Art Archive/Courtauld Institute London/Superstock, (bottom) The Art Archive/Museo del Prado Madrid; p2: Ellen DeGeneres/Twitter via Getty Images; p4: The Art Archive/Courtauld Institute London/Superstock; p5: Fabio Lamanna/Shutterstock.com; p6: The Art Archive/DeA Picture Library; p7: (top) The Art Archive/Egyptian Museum, Berlin/Werner Forman Archive, (bottom) Frater Rufillus/Wikicommons; p8: The Art Archive/National Gallery London/Eileen Tweedy; p9: The Art Archive/National Gallery London/Eileen Tweedy; p10: The Art Archive/Museo del Prado Madrid; p11: The Art Archive/Bibliothèque des Arts Décoratifs Paris/Gianni Dagli Orti; p12: The Art Archive/Room of the Segnature, Vatican Palace, Vatican Museum, Vatican City/Mondadori Portfolio/Electa; p13: The Art Archive/Sistine Chapel Vatican/Superstock; p14: The Art Archive/Private Collection Italy/Gianni Dagli Orti; p16: The Art Archive/Museo del Prado Madrid/Gianni Dagli Orti; p17: (left) The Art Archive/Royal Collection/Superstock/Fine Art Images, (right) The Art Archive/Pinacoteca di Brera, Milan/Mondadori Portfolio/Electa; p18: (top) The Art Archive/DeA Picture Library/E. Lessing, (bottom) The Art Archive/National Gallery London/Eileen Tweedy; p19: The Art Archive/Galleria degli Uffizi Florence/Collection Dagli Orti; p20: The Art Archive National Gallery London/Eileen Tweedy; p21: The Art Archive/National Gallery London/Eileen Tweedy; p22: Self-Portrait, Yawning, 1783 (oil on canvas), Ducreux, Joseph (1735-1802)/J. Paul Getty Museum, Los Angeles, USA/Bridgeman Images; p23: The Art Archive/Slovak National Gallery, Bratislava/Superstock; p24: The Art Archive/Musée Fabre Montpelier/Gianni Dagli Orti; p26: Wikicommons; p27: Wikicommons; p29: The Art Archive/Courtauld Institute London/Superstock; p30: The Art Archive/Private Collection/Gianni Dagli Orti, All rights reserved. DACS 2015.; p32: Self-Portrait, 1907 (oil on canvas), Picasso, Pablo (1881-1973)/Národní Galerie, Prague, Czech Republic/Bridgeman Images. All rights reserved. DACS 2015.; p33: Sergey Uryadnikov/Shutterstock.com; p35: The Art Archive/DeA Picture Library/E. Lessing. All rights reserved. DACS 2015.; p36: The Art Archive/Museum of Modern Art Mexico/Gianni Dagli Orti. All rights reserved. DACS 2015.; p37: The Art Archive/Gianni Dagli Orti. All rights reserved. DACS 2015.; p38: Self-Portrait at the Mirror, Parmigianino (Francesco Mazzola) (1503-40)/Kunsthistorisches Museum, Vienna, Austria/Ali Meyer/Bridgeman Images; p39: The Art Archive/Thyssen-Bornemisza Museum, Madrid, Spain/Mondadori Portfolio/Electa. © The Lucian Freud Archive/Bridgeman Images; p40: The Art Archive/Private Collection Paris © The Estate of Francis Bacon. All rights reserved. DACS 2015.; p43: The Art Archive/The Solomon R. Guggenheim Foundation/Art Resource, NY/Solomon R. Guggenheim Museum, New York. Gift, Anne and Anthony d'Offay in honor of Thomas Krens, 1992. All rights reserved. DACS 2015.; p44: Ellen DeGeneres/Twitter via Getty Images; p45: (top) FILIPPO MONTEFORTE/AFP/Getty Images; (bottom) Wikicommons

Contents

All By Your Selfie

You can probably do it with your eyes closed: hold your phone at arm's length; point the camera at your face; press the shutter button; bingo – a selfie! So next time you smile/hug a celebrity and post the pic on Instagram, spare a thought for Leonardo da Vinci, Albrecht Dürer, Frida Kahlo, Rembrandt van Rijn, Diego Velázquez and Vincent van Gogh among others. They never saw a smartphone, or the Internet or any form of social networking. Most of them couldn't even tell you what a camera was. But they did all know about selfies!

Vincent van Gogh: Self-Portrait with Bandaged Ear, 1889

Back in the old days, the word 'selfie' wasn't exactly in fashion – 'SELF-PORTRAIT' was the traditional way of saying it. Before photography was invented, people who wanted to look at pictures of themselves (and could afford to) commissioned artists to paint their portraits. If you were an artist it was even easier – you just looked in the mirror and painted what you saw!

It didn't stop when photography appeared. Over the years, all kinds of artists have discovered that one of the handiest, most fascinating subjects of all is sitting right there, in their very own skin.

Self-Portrait of Unknown Man, 2015

Self-portraits can often tell us about the clothing of a particular time, about art materials and styles, and how old or rich or handsome the artist was or is — but most of all they let us look right inside the brilliant (and sometimes a bit bonkers) people who created them.

Take Vincent van Gogh, who famously cut off a piece of his ear but still thought it would make a nice picture. Rembrandt drew, painted and etched his own reflection so many times we can see almost every stage of his life! Some modern artists have painted or sculpted their feelings through strange colours or abstract shapes without even a face to recognize.

There's a whole world of creative characters packed inside this book, all shown just as they wanted you to see them. Every selfie tells a story — so put down your mobile, switch off the webcam and read on!

Selfies of Old

Some selfies are seriously ancient. As many as FORTY THOUSAND years ago, people were making a type of self-image by stencilling their own hands on cave walls.

Most Stone Age hand stencils seem to be left hands, suggesting the artists used their right hand to paint. They would press a palm onto the wall, then blow paint through a hollow reed or bone (or just spit a mouthful of it!) around the shape. Hand stencils were made by men, women and children. The oldest found are on the island of Sulawesi in Indonesia.

Cave paintings in Patagonia, Argentina, c7000 BCE

In Ancient Egypt, artists took selfies a step further and carved their faces and figures in stone. Some of the earliest examples are by Bak, chief sculptor to the Pharaoh Akhenaten. Bak was proud of his successful career, as we can see in this self-portrait with his wife (right). He is the one with the gigantic belly, revealing to everyone that he's rich enough to enjoy a good feast.

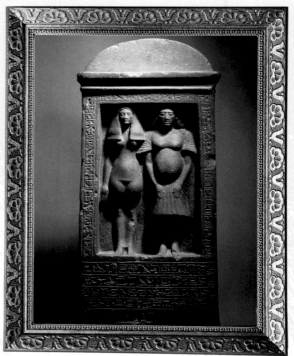

Bak, Self-Portrait with his Wife, Taheri, c1353-1336 BCE

Brother Rufillus, Self-Portrait Illuminating the Initial 'R', c1170-1200

By the Middle Ages, artists in Europe were painting self-portraits into decorative illuminated manuscripts. The printing press hadn't been invented yet, so these texts were written and illustrated by hand — often by monks in monasteries. In the picture above, we can see Brother Rufillus of Weissenau, busy working on the initial letter of his name. He has turned the leg of the 'R' into a serpent and added other mythical creatures around it.

If the Greek historian Plutarch is to be believed, one ancient selfie put its maker in prison! In around 447 BCE, the sculptor Phidias made a statue of the goddess Athena for the Parthenon temple in Athens. Unfortunately he carved his own face on her shield — and was locked away for being vain and disrespectful!

Nowadays artists have a huge range of paint colours to choose from — but cave painters relied on simple natural pigments such as clay ochre, charcoal or burnt bones. Medieval artists also used earth, plant and animal extracts as their colours. They would mix them with a binder such as egg white and water, and sometimes honey or earwax!

Jan van Eyck

Portrait of a Man (Self-Portrait?), 1433

Born: 1390 in Belgium (though was Dutch)
Died: 1441, aged 51

Why is the man in the red turban staring straight towards us? He might be looking in a mirror, studying his own face. Most experts think that this painting is a self-portrait, because of the focussed expression and the angle of the eyes. Another clue is in van Eyck's name and motto, which he wrote in big letters on the picture's frame.

This could be the first independent self-portrait, but why did van Eyck paint it? One theory is that he wanted to show off his skill — if he took the picture to his clients in person, they could see what a remarkable likeness it was. On the other hand, van Eyck was already a respected portrait artist, so perhaps he just painted this to give to someone, or because he had some spare time!

Van Eyck worked in oil paints, so brilliantly that people thought he invented them! In fact oil painting was nothing new at the time, but he helped it to become the next big thing in Europe. Oil paints dry slowly, allowing artists to blend them and build up layers of rich, glowing colour. Van Eyck was a master at painting incredible, realistic detail, from the stubble on his chin to his shiny, bloodshot eyes.

People used to polish stone or metal (or look in water) to see their reflections. Glass mirrors were around in van Eyck's day, but they were small and usually curved. In the 16th century, glass-makers in Venice, Italy, found a way to make clear, flat mirrors with a tin-mercury backing. The silvered-glass mirrors that we use today weren't invented until 1835.

The Arnolfini Portrait, 1434

This famous painting by van Eyck might also contain a selfie. Look at the mirror on the back wall – one of the reflected figures, standing in the doorway, is thought to be the artist himself. He even wrote above the mirror: 'Jan van Eyck was here'!

Albrecht Dürer

Dürer looks haughty and confident, with a stiff but elegant pose.

His clothing is expensive, extravagant and Italian in style.

Born: 1471 in Germany
Died: 1528, aged 56

Self-Portrait, 1500

Dürer signed all his work with the monogram AD.

We all want to look good in a selfie — and 500 years ago it was the same. Albrecht Dürer groomed his hair and dressed up in fancy clothes for this self-portrait, announcing to the world that he was somebody rich and grand.

Dürer was 26 when he painted this. He was already a leading artist, best known for his woodcut prints. On a recent trip to Italy, he had noticed that great artists had a higher social status than they did at home in Germany. Dürer wanted to be treated like that too!

Look at the amazing detail in Dürer's corkscrew curls. He put a lot of effort into painting every strand of his tumbling hair, moustache and beard. The Italian artist, Giovanni Bellini (c.1430–1516) was so impressed with the way Dürer painted hair that he asked to see one of his special brushes. Of course, there was nothing special about his brushes at all!

Dürer was one of the first artists to make a series of self-portraits. His first was a silverpoint drawing, done at the age of 13 when he was training as a goldsmith in his father's jewellery shop. Some time later he wrote proudly on the picture: '*This I have drawn from myself from the looking glass, in the year 1484, when I was still a child* — Albrecht Dürer.'

Self-Portrait, Engraving After Drawing, 1494

After Dürer's death, admirers cut locks of his hair to remember him by — you can still see some at the Academy of Fine Arts in Vienna, Austria!

Selfies in Disguise

Selfie sticks weren't around hundreds of years ago, but artists could still picture themselves in a group scene. During a time called the Renaissance*, huge classical or religious paintings were all the rage – and artists were their own handiest models.

The School of Athens, 1509-11

Raphael   Michelangelo   Leonardo da Vinci

Raphael
Born: 1483 in Italy
Died: 1520, aged 37

In 1508, the young Italian painter Raphael was commissioned to decorate several rooms at the Vatican in Rome. One of them was the Pope's library, where he began *The School of Athens* in 1509. It's a fresco, which means it is painted directly onto wet plaster on the wall. The scene is set in Ancient Greece and shows a whole range of great thinkers, from writers and philosophers to scientists and mathematicians.

* This was a period of great creativity in Europe, from the 14th-16th centuries. Artists revived ideas from classical antiquity – in other words, Ancient Greece and Rome.

Raphael snuck himself in as a student in this huge painting. He's standing with the astronomers Ptolemy and Zoroaster, who are both holding globes. Several other figures are modelled on artists that Raphael knew – including his two greatest rivals. The philosopher Plato has the face of Leonardo da Vinci (see pp14–15), while Heraclitus is Michelangelo in disguise.

While Raphael was busy at the Vatican, Michelangelo was also working there. He was decorating the ceiling of the Sistine Chapel, where he later painted a wall with a scene called *The Last Judgement*. In this gigantic fresco, Michelangelo included his own self-portrait – on the crumpled, flayed skin of St Bartholomew. It's about as ghoulish as a selfie can be.

Saint Bartholomew with his Flayed Skin (detail from The Last Judgement), 1536-41

Born: 1475 in Italy
Died: 1564, aged 88

Some other Renaissance selfies in disguise...

Piero della Francesca – as a sleeping soldier in *The Resurrection*, c1460

Sandro Botticelli – as a bystander in *Adoration of the Magi*, 1475–76

Paolo Veronese – as a violinist in *The Marriage at Cana*, 1562

Leonardo da Vinci

Portrait of a Man in Red
Chalk, 1512

Born: 1452 in Italy
Died: 1519, aged 67

With all the photos and websites around today, we can usually find out what someone looks like. But how do we recognize people from the past? Sometimes it's hard to know for sure if a painting or drawing is actually who we think it is – and that is the case with this picture.

Most people agree that this red chalk drawing is by Leonardo da Vinci. It dates to his lifetime and shows the delicate lines and shading that he was famous for. Experts can also tell that it was drawn with a left hand – and Leonardo was left-handed. People who wrote about him described his striking looks and, in later life, his long hair and flowing beard. There are portraits, thought to be of him, that fit this description too.

The date of this drawing would make Leonardo about 60. The problem is, he looks a lot older! Some people believe that he looked old for his age or that he deliberately drew himself as a wise, elderly man. Others suggest that this might be his father or uncle, who both lived until they were 80.

Leonardo da Vinci was a great painter, sculptor, scientist, inventor and basically an all-round genius. He filled sketchbooks with designs for flying machines, musical instruments and other devices that were way ahead of his time. His studies of the human body are extraordinarily detailed, down to the tiniest veins and bones – he learned by cutting up corpses and copying them.

Leonardo wrote in mirror writing, from right to left across the page. Because he was left-handed, some people say this was to stop him smudging the ink. Others believe it was a type of code, hiding his ideas from nosy readers, or competitors.

Las Meninas, 1656

Born: 1599 in Spain
Died: 1660, aged 61

It's easy to spot the artist in this picture – he's the one with the brush and palette in his hand! Velázquez was working as a court painter for the Spanish royal family, but what is he painting here? We can only guess what's on the canvas propped in front of him.

There is a clue at the back of the picture. Can you see a big mirror on the wall? It shows the reflection of two people – they must be standing where we are, facing Velázquez, perhaps posing for their portraits to be painted. Our eye is drawn towards them by the shapes of the other figures, and by the triangle of light in the scene. Who are the two people? The king and queen!

Nearly everyone in the painting is looking towards us — well actually, towards the royal couple. In the centre is the five-year-old princess, being fussed over by her meninas, or ladies-in-waiting. Velázquez is hovering in the shadows, but the enormous canvas he is painting stands out and reminds us of his importance. The artist had his own rooms in the royal palace, and he set this one up as a studio where the king would often watch him work.

Many other famous artists have painted self-portraits that show the tools of their trade. Here are just a few...

Pieter Brueghel the Elder *The Painter and the Buyer*, 1565
Jan Vermeer *The Artist's Studio*, 1665–68
Joshua Reynolds *Self-Portrait*, 1747–48
Paul Gauguin *Self-Portrait with Palette*, c1883/84
Paul Cézanne *Self-Portrait with Palette*, 1885–87

Self-Portrait as the Allegory of Painting, 1638-39

Artemisia Gentileschi
Born: 1593 in Italy
Died: c1652, aged c59

Self-Portrait, 1906

Umberto Boccioni
Born: 1882 in Italy
Died: 1916, aged 33

Rembrandt van Rijn

He wasn't quite Kim Kardashian, but Rembrandt was the biggest selfie maker of his time. He created nearly 100 self-portraits, spanning 40 years of his life. They give us a kind of diary in pictures, tracking his changing appearance as well as his developing painting style.

Rembrandt began training as a painter in his teens, and quickly became a massive success. Many important people in his home country, the Netherlands, commissioned him to paint. But later he became bankrupt, and suffered from the death of his wife, son and other loved ones. It helps to explain the emotion that we see in his final self-portrait (right).

Self-Portrait as a Young Man, 1634

Rembrandt liked to vary his selfies — he pictured himself in all sorts of different poses, outfits and moods. As a young man, he often appeared in fine clothing, perhaps in the style of the rich people whose portraits he painted. Sometimes his scenes were theatrical, like this one below at the age of 29 with his wife Saskia sitting on his knee.

By the end of his life, Rembrandt knew his face pretty well. He was also an expert at capturing character. He stripped away all the fancy dress and showed us simply Rembrandt the person. In his last self-portrait aged 63, he seems sad yet calm and dignified. We see him inside and out, with every lump, sag and wrinkle on display.

Self-Portrait with Saskia, 1636

Born: 1606 in the Netherlands
Died: 1669, aged 63

When experts examined this painting under X-ray, they discovered that the artist had made some changes. Originally his hat was much bigger and all white, and his hands had held a paintbrush. Rembrandt painted over this detail, bringing all our attention back to his face.

Elizabeth Vigée Le Brun

This lady looks pretty in her feathered straw hat and pink dress. She has a gentle smile and a friendly gaze and holds open a welcoming hand. Vigée Le Brun wanted people to look at her and like her in this selfie — and that's exactly what they did.

The straw hat self-portrait was an instant hit for Vigée Le Brun – she even made copies, as she did with other paintings, for her admirers. It made her such a name that she was admitted to the French Royal Academy of Art. This was a great achievement, as only four women were allowed to be members at the time.

In the 18th century, when Vigée Le Brun was painting, female artists had to work hard to be taken seriously. Traditionally painting was a man's world, and something that women mostly did as a hobby. Vigée Le Brun was extremely talented and she also sold her skills well. Self-portraits like this one were a way to attract attention and win people's hearts.

Born: 1755 in France
Died: 1842, aged 86

Self-Portrait in a Straw Hat, 1782

Elizabeth looks natural and relaxed in the painting, with her untamed hair and loose clothes. She seems comfortable with her palette and brushes, but they aren't the focus of the scene.

For people in the art world, there was something familiar about this work — it was modelled on a portrait by Peter Paul Rubens, done over a hundred years before. Vigée Le Brun was a big fan of Rubens, so she set herself a challenge to paint in his famous style.

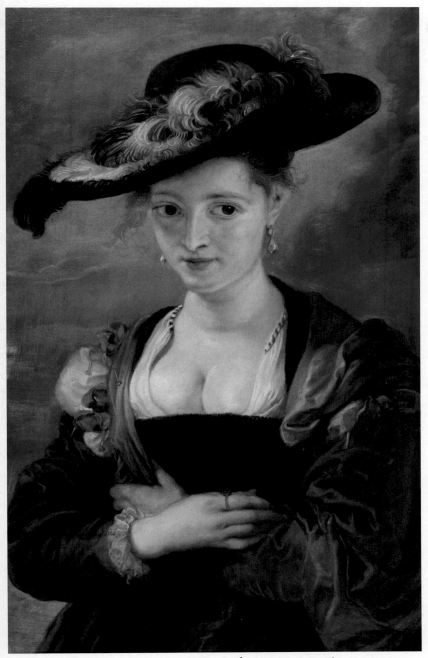

Portrait of Susanna Lunden, 1622-1625

Vigée Le Brun made a living from her portraits from an early age. As her reputation grew, she caught the eye of many wealthy people, including the French queen, Marie Antoinette. Vigée Le Brun painted her more than 20 times, and made a selfie showing herself working on a portrait of the queen. When the film *Marie Antoinette* was made in 2006, Vigée Le Brun was featured in it!

Peter Paul Rubens
Born: 1577 in Germany
Died: 1640, aged 62

These days, funny faces in selfies are nothing unusual (think 'duckface'!), but in the 1700s people tended to be more straight-faced. Most self-portraits had a neutral expression, avoiding any strong feeling of being happy, cross or tired. It was different for the artists on these pages, though!

Joseph Ducreux found traditional portraiture a bit too prim and proper. He studied the way people's faces reflected their character, and tried to capture the personalities of everyone he painted. In this self-portrait, he caught himself right in the middle of a yawn, screwing up his face and stretching. There's nothing shy or self-conscious about it — he pushes out his belly and opens his mouth wide, in a way that makes us want to yawn too.

Self-Portrait, Yawning, 1783

Joseph Ducreux
Born: 1735 in France
Died: 1802, aged 67

Ducreux painted many other funny and expressive portraits. Today, more than 200 years after his death, his selfies are all over the Internet! Ducreux has at least two Twitter feeds and a long-running meme, where people caption his pictures with jokey, old-fashioned hip-hop lyrics. Fans have even made t-shirts, animations and 3D printed versions of his work.

The sculptor Franz Xaver Messerschmidt pinched himself in front of a mirror to record his changing expressions! He turned his gruesome grimaces into 64 'character heads', carving them in stone or wood or casting them in metal. Some reports say that Messerschmidt, who was growing increasingly eccentric, made the heads to scare away ghosts and spirits that tormented him at night.

Ten years after Messerschmidt's death, there was an exhibition of his character heads in Vienna, Austria, where he had once lived. The organizers gave the heads descriptive titles, including *Just Rescued from Drowning*, *The Incapable Bassoonist* and *Childish Weeping*! This one, *The Big Secret*, shows the face you might pull if you've just revealed or heard someone's secret, or are trying very hard to keep one.

Franz Xaver Messerschmidt
Born: 1736 in Germany
Died: 1783, aged 47

The Big Secret, 1770-1783

Gustave Courbet

The painter of this selfie called himself 'the proudest and most arrogant man in France'! Can you tell which of these three figures is him? There are clues in the things he is carrying — and also in the way he has arranged the scene.

The Meeting, or Hello Mr Courbet, 1854

Born: 1819 in France
Died: 1877, aged 58

Who is the biggest and most prominent person? It's the man on the right, with a pointy beard. He is the artist, Gustave Courbet. On his back he carries a fold-up easel and a box of paints, with a canvas rolled on the top. He is standing in full sunlight, while the other two men are under the shadow of a tree.

Critics at the time called this a boastful painting. They laughed at the way Courbet had made such a pompous picture out of an ordinary, trivial meeting. People were used to seeing characters from the Bible, myths or history in storytelling paintings like this. The bumptious Courbet was lifting an everyday experience to a new, important level!

So who are the other two figures? The man in green is Alfred Bruyas — a buyer and supporter of Courbet's work. Next to him is his servant, Calas. All three men have taken off their hats to greet each other, but while Calas bows and Bruyas lowers his eyes, Courbet tips his head back confidently. He seems to be the one with the upper hand, dressed for the country and carrying all the equipment he needs. Even the dog is standing to attention, looking up as if listening to Courbet!

Courbet may have shocked people with his attitude, but he helped to set a new trend in painting. He said he wanted to create 'living art', showing scenes of his time that he knew and understood. He painted workers in fields and peasants at a funeral. Instead of dressing things up, he showed the truth of everyday life. His style became known as Realism.

Courbet painted other attention-grabbing self-portraits – he said they told the story of his changing states of mind. In one we see him up-close, clutching his head and looking terrified. In another he lies heroic and wounded with a bullet through his heart.

The First Photos

When the first fixed photograph, or daguerrotype, was released, people reacted with amazement, excitement and even fear! This extraordinary invention took a while to reach ordinary households, but when it did the snapshot selfie took off.

The daguerrotype was unveiled in 1839, by the Frenchman Louis Daguerre. It involved a simple box camera that produced a picture on a light-sensitive metal plate. People soon dreamed up variations on this idea, and about 50 years later the first camera using film went on sale. The 'Kodak' was small and easy to use, and people could take 100 pictures before sending it back to the factory for processing.

Self-Portrait of an Unidentified Lady, 1900

In 1900, a whole new world was opened up by the Kodak Brownie — a very cheap and very popular portable camera. Now anyone could take a selfie, though they didn't have screens, autofocus or self-timers! Like this Edwardian lady, they would usually pose in front of a mirror and prop the camera on a table to keep it steady. The viewfinder was on top of the box, so the trick was to hold it at waist height and look down to compose the shot.

The Grand Duchess Anastasia Nikolaevna of Russia took one of the first teen selfies with a Kodak Brownie. She sent it to a friend, with a letter saying that it was hard to take because her hands were shaking! The Brownie was marketed at children and young people – there was even a Brownie Camera Club, offering prizes for the best pictures.

The word photography means 'drawing with light', and in the 19th century it wasn't a new idea. It developed from the camera obscura, a device that had been around since ancient times. The camera obscura projected an image onto a surface, but to keep it you had to draw over it. The image came out upside-down, until mirrors and lenses were used to correct this.

Anastasia Nikolaevna, 1914

The invention of photography had a big impact on art, especially portrait painting. There was now a far quicker and cheaper way to get a picture of a person. Some artists resented the competition, while others used photographs to help their work. Painting became more experimental, moving beyond just a realistic likeness.

Vincent van Gogh

You might take a selfie when something unusual happens to you. Van Gogh made this one soon after he cut a piece from his ear! It followed an argument with his friend and fellow artist, Gauguin.

Can you see the bandage on the side of van Gogh's head? The unlucky ear was actually the left one, but of course he was looking in a mirror when he painted this. Rather than turning to hide his injury, he made it the focus of the picture. His face looks still and serious, as if he's lost in thought.

Why is van Gogh wearing a hat and coat? Perhaps there's a draught coming in through the blue window. It was wintertime, and the house in france where he lived and worked wouldn't have had central heating. The room is filled with a chilly yellow-green light that gives his skin a sickly feel. Van Gogh was poor and often spent his money on paint instead of food.

Van Gogh made more than 850 paintings in just 10 years, but he managed to sell only one in his lifetime. Now he's one of the most famous artists in history and collectors pay many millions for his work!

Notice how van Gogh painted using big, thick brushstrokes. They bring out the different textures of his clothes, fur cap, bandage and bony face. Sometimes he squeezed paint straight from the tube onto the canvas, and it would take weeks and weeks to dry! Behind the artist we can see a canvas — what is he going to paint on it? To the other side is a copy of a Japanese print. Van Gogh was fascinated by Japanese art. He loved its bold outlines, flat colours and decorative shapes, and did his best to use them in his own work.

When he painted this selfie, van Gogh was mentally ill. After cutting the chunk off his ear, he gave it to a woman as a 'gift'. He was taken into hospital and a few months later checked into an asylum. Although he continued to paint, he was unable to recover and shot himself the following year.

Self-Portrait with
Bandaged Ear, 1889

Born: 1853 in Netherlands
Died: 1890, aged 37

*Self-Portrait Surrounded
by Masks, 1899*

Born: 1860 in Belgium
Died: 1949, aged 89

There's something spooky about this selfie, staring out from a sea of masks. What is James Ensor doing here, dressed in a lady's hat? Is he trapped among the masks or is he controlling them? Is the scene real, or imagined like a dream or a nightmare?

Look at the faces on the masks. They are brightly painted, like clowns. Some stare, some grin and others gawp with open mouths. Are they teasing Ensor or are they his friends? It's hard to tell.

Masks were a popular theme with Ensor — his family stocked them in their souvenir shop, ready for the annual carnival. Ensor loved visiting puppet theatres and reading fantasy stories too. He painted masks and skeletons over and over again, and many people criticized his work. That was fine by Ensor, who once wrote to a friend: 'I liked these masks, because they offended the public who had given me such a poor reception.'

Ensor painted 112 self-portraits. Even so, he declared, 'I've never managed to capture the resemblance.' He put himself in some strange and sometimes comical disguises — in one picture, his severed head is on a platter, being served to a table of critics!

Why the feathered hat? Again we can't be certain, though costume was nothing new in the world of self-portraits. It reminds us of the hat worn by Vigée Le Brun (see pp20–21) and also the way Rembrandt (pp18–19) dressed up. Ensor had painted himself in a similar hat over ten years before, but then it was green with coloured flowers.

Ensor rarely left his birthplace of Ostend in Belgium. He worked in an attic studio above his parents' shop. Although it took people a while to accept his unusual paintings, he became a respected artist in his time. He also helped to influence the art of the future, especially Expressionism (see p34) and Surrealism.

Pablo Picasso

This face seems quite ungainly with its thick lines, scribbled colours and jagged shapes. It looks almost like a mask, carved roughly out of wood. That tells us something about Picasso's inspiration – he had just discovered African sculpture, including tribal masks!

Self-Portrait, 1907

Born: 1881 in Spain
Died: 1973, aged 91

Picasso was a gifted artist who knew perfectly well how to draw a realistic face. But he deliberately simplified his features here. His eyes are wide, flat, almond shapes and his nose and cheekbones are shown by minimal lines. Picasso used chunky brushstrokes and didn't try to recreate the softness of skin, clothes or hair.

At this stage in his career, Picasso was on the verge of developing a new art movement (though he may not have known it yet). The movement became known as Cubism, and it was a way of representing the world as a jumble of geometric shapes.

Cubist artists blended different viewpoints, so parts of a picture might look face-on, others from above and others from the left or right. You'll notice signs of this in the painting on p32, with the ear seen from the side and the eyes from the front.

Picasso loved African art. He discovered it in museums in Paris where he worked, and built up a huge collection of masks, such as this one, and sculptures. They inspired him for much of his life, but especially between the years of 1907 and 1909, which became known as his 'African Period'.

African Tribal Mask, date unknown

During his career, Picasso experimented with many different art styles and his self-portraits are really varied. Some are realistic, some are spooky, some are serious and others are funny. He drew himself as a monkey, and another time cut out a photo of his eyes and stuck them to a sketch of an owl! Picasso loved animals and kept a lot of pets, including a sausage dog called Lump.

Oscar Kokoschka

It's hard to feel happy when you look at this painting – everything about it seems uncomfortable and distressing. The man looks sad and anxious, with his down-turned lips and a hand raised to his face. Kokoschka was excellent at painting powerful emotion.

When he made this self-portrait, Kokoschka was in a sorry state. A few years earlier, the love of his life had left him and he had volunteered for military service in World War I. Kokoschka was shot in the head and stabbed in the chest, and was later diagnosed with shell-shock (a mental illness). He travelled to Dresden, Germany, to recover.

When Kokoschka's girlfriend left him, he missed her so much that he had a life-size doll made of her! He used this as a model to draw and paint from in his studio.

In this painting, Kokoschka's eyebrows are raised and worried over his dark, hollow eyes. He looks back over his shoulder in an awkward, unbalanced pose and his hand touches his lips in a nervous gesture. The paint is thick, slapped on with heavy brushstrokes, and there are lots of blues, greys and greens, which are cold colours. The greenish yellow of Kokoschka's face makes him look unwell.

Expressionist paintings weren't all sad – some were filled with warm, cheerful colours such as reds, oranges and yellows. One group of artists used such bright and wacky colours that they were nicknamed the Fauves, or 'wild beasts'.

Kokoschka's painting style was known as Expressionism – because it expressed strong feelings. It was an idea that grew up in Germany at the turn of the 20th century. Expressionist artists wanted to show what was on the inside, rather than how things looked on the surface. To get this across, they exaggerated shapes and colours, and painted with big, agitated brushstrokes.

Self-Portrait, One Hand Touching the Face, 1918

Born: 1886 in Austria
Died: 1980, aged 93

Kahlo & Rivera

One woman sits with a bleeding heart, while her identical twin holds her hand. In fact these are both the same person – Frida Kahlo. She had recently been divorced from Diego Rivera, the artist who painted the scene on p37.

The Two Fridas, 1939

The Frida on the right is holding a miniature portrait of Diego. A vein runs all the way from this picture, through both Fridas' hearts, to the place where it drips on her white dress. Although the Frida on the left is hurt, she looks calm and strengthened by the figure next to her. They don't seem to notice the dismal storm brewing behind.

Frida Kahlo
Born: 1907 in Mexico
Died: 1954, aged 47

ahli was badly affected by childhood polio and severe injuries from a bus crash at the age of 18. To cover up her impediments, she designed her own clothing with colourful long skirts and supportive corsets. She suffered physical and emotional pain all her life, and expressed this in her work — especially self-portraits like this one.

Dream of a Sunday Afternoon in Alameda Park (detail), 1947

Diego Rivera
Born: 1886 in Mexico
Died: 1957, aged 70

Kahlo took up painting while she was recovering in hospital after her accident. She had to wear full body casts, which she decorated brightly with her paints. When her lower leg was amputated, she designed her own prosthetic one, dressed in a fancy red boot with a bell on it!

iego Rivera included himself and Frida in a gigantic wall painting showing scenes from the history of Mexico. Of course he was grown-up at the time, but in the mural he's a boy with a frog and snake in his pockets! Frida is right behind him, resting a hand on his shoulder. In her other hand she holds a Yin and Yang symbol, representing the differences between her and Diego.

Kahlo and Rivera couldn't make up their minds about each other — they got married, divorced, then married again! When Kahlo died, Rivera ordered all her clothes to be locked away until 15 years after he died too. They were rediscovered only in 2004.

Weird Reflections

What happens if you take a selfie from up high or down low? You might find you look out of shape. Lucian Freud painted this self-portrait (right) using a mirror that was flat on the floor. It's hard to make sense of the picture at first.

If you look carefully, you'll notice the edge of the mirror at the bottom of the painting. Freud is looming over it with his eyes peering down towards his feet. The grey area around him is the ceiling, not a wall – you can see the round shapes of two hanging lights, as if we're looking up at them from underneath.

Looking at the painting makes us feel a bit off-balance. Freud swirled in the background using a palette knife (like a narrow metal spatula) instead of a brush. His face is lit up against the grey, looking strained as he squints downwards. And what about the children? They seem tiny compared to the giant man next to them.

Many artists have played with weird reflections. One of the first was Parmigianino, who painted his reflection in a curved mirror, on a curved wooden panel, in 1524 when he was 21!

Parmigianino
Born: 1503 in Italy
Died: 1540, aged 37

Self-Portrait in a Convex Mirror, 1524

The children are Freud's daughter, Rose, and son, Ali. They're not reflected in the mirror, and they don't seem to be lying on the floor. If they're sitting up in front of him, they are unrealistically small. Freud is messing with the way we see things, mixing different viewpoints and playing with scale. He was inspired by the carved stone tomb of a dwarf, Seneb, and his family in Egypt, which shows two tiny children in front of their much larger parents.

Reflection with Two Children
(Self-Portrait), 1965

Born: 1922 in Germany (though was British)
Died: 2011, aged 88

Francis Bacon

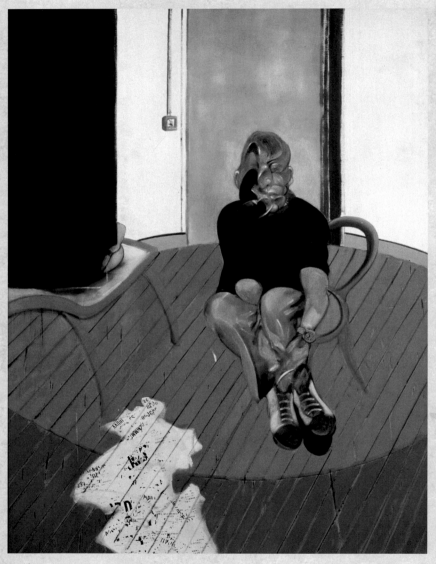

Self-Portrait, 1973

Born: 1909 in Ireland
Died: 1992, aged 82

It would be tricky to recognize this man from his face — it's all blurred and twisted out of shape! Francis Bacon didn't copy exactly what he saw in the mirror, but he had such a distinctive style of painting that we can tell straight away it is him.

Bacon liked to distort things without hiding his appearance altogether. This figure isn't completely abstract – we can see an arm, knees and two clearly painted feet, and his face is partly visible. A lot of the background makes sense too, with the familiar shape of a chair, a door and a light switch. Bacon has painted diagonal floorboards and the oval beam from a light, to show there is space in the room. But other parts of the picture are puzzling.

Bacon largely taught himself to paint, and he didn't only use brushes. Sometimes he would throw paint at the canvas, smudge it with a rag or use his fingers. If he felt like it, he would mix sand or dirt with the paint to create texture, or blend oil paints with pastels for different effects.

Like the Expressionists (see p34), Bacon chose to look at himself from the inside. He was a lively character, but he had quite a gloomy outlook on life. His self-portraits are often haunting, showing him as a lonely figure with a ghostly or monster-like head. He painted other people in a similar way, including his friend and rival Lucian Freud (p39).

Bacon worked in a famously messy studio, exploding with paint pots and colours that he tested on the walls. After his death, it was moved (walls and all) to a museum in Dublin, Ireland. There were 7,000 items in that studio! Experts took photos and made drawings and maps so that they could reconstruct it perfectly, piece by piece.

In 2013, a triple portrait of Lucian Freud by Francis Bacon sold at auction for US$142 million – a record-busting price at the time!

Andy Warhol

Imagine this green face at its actual size – about eight times the size of this book! It would make quite an impact hanging on a wall, and Andy Warhol was all about IMPACT.

Lots of things are striking about this larger-than-life picture. For a start, Warhol used only two colours. Green is a peculiar choice for a face, but it glows out impressively against the black. Andy Warhol's body is missing, so the head floats freakishly in space. His hair shoots upwards and outwards with a life of its own – it is actually his trademark wig.

It seems as if the artist is showing off here, as if he's flashing his face in neon lights. Warhol loved fame and celebrity, film stars, brand names and advertising images. Anything that was eye-catching and modern, he was ready to turn it into art. His obsession with popular culture gave his style the name 'Pop Art'.

Warhol often made multiple images, repeating the same face in one artwork. He even created a self-portrait wallpaper! His studio was nicknamed 'The Factory' because of all the prints and paintings it churned out.

Warhol created this selfie in different colours too – in red, pink, blue, white and even a camouflage pattern. He used a method called silkscreen printing, which involved pushing ink through a type of stencil. Warhol liked the fact that he could reproduce images, just as the images on billboards and packaging were reproduced. He wasn't bothered about the personal touch, saying: 'I think somebody should be able to do all my paintings for me.'

Born: 1928 in America
Died: 1987, aged 58

Self-Portrait, 1986

Warhol died the year after he made this selfie, but by then he was a celebrity himself. He had been an illustrator, artist, filmmaker, photographer, writer and even a rock band manager! Warhol said that in the future everyone would be famous for 15 minutes, but his fame has lasted far longer than that. Nowadays it's easy to find a computer program that will turn your photo into a Warhol-style artwork.

Selfies Today

Selfies today are everywhere! With the invention of digital cameras and smartphones, anyone can snap themselves in an instant and share the picture with their friends or the world. Celebrities are doing it. Politicians are doing it. Even animals are doing it (sort of)! Will the selfie craze ever end?

2013 was the year that '#selfie' took off. More than 17 million people were posting a selfie on social media every week. In 2014, the word 'selfie' made it into the Oxford Dictionary and was approved for the board game Scrabble! Technologies such as front-facing cameras, selfie sticks and hand-gesture sensors have made selfie-snapping easier than ever before.

Perhaps the most famous selfie ever was taken at the Oscars in 2014, showing a gaggle of glamorous stars. Within 24 hours it was retweeted 2.8 million times, breaking the previous record held by US President Barack Obama after his 2012 election win!

Oscar selfie, 2014

Pope Francis, 2014

In 2013, Pope Francis went viral in the first 'Papal selfie', taken with young fans at the Vatican.

Self-Portrait of a female Celebes crested macaque, 2011

This cheeky monkey in Indonesia ran off with a wildlife photographer's camera and took several crystal-clear selfies! Whether she meant to do it or not, we're not sure...

Modern artists have had some wacky ideas to capture their own image in ways that a camera can't. For example, the Bahamas-born Janine Antoni made a series of selfie sculptures out of chocolate and soap, then 'resculpted' them by licking the chocolate and bathing with the soap!

When you post a selfie, you're displaying a view of yourself that you want other people to see. When artists make self-portraits, it's the same! So next time you pose and click the camera on your smartphone, remember you have something in common with every famous face in this book!

Glossary

abstract not showing the actual appearance of an object, place or living thing. Abstract art often focuses on simplified lines, shapes, colours or use of space.

auction a sale where people bid for items and the person offering the highest bid wins

camera obscura a darkened box with a hole in one side, which projects an image of something outside the box onto a surface inside

canvas a strong type of fabric that can be stretched across a frame for artists to paint on

carve to cut into a material such as wood or stone, creating a 3D image

cast to produce a sculpture by pouring hot molten metal into a mould

charcoal a black substance, produced by heating wood, bone or other natural materials without any oxygen present. Artists can use charcoal to draw with.

classical relating to Ancient Greek or Roman art, literature or culture

commission to pay someone to produce something, such as a portrait or other painting

Cubism an art style (1907–1920s) in which artists made images using geometric shapes and multiple viewpoints

daguerrotype an early type of photograph, produced on a highly polished, silver-treated sheet of copper

easel a wooden stand that supports an artist's canvas or drawing board

etch to engrave a design onto glass, stone or metal, using an acid to cut into the lines. A print can then be made by spreading ink over the design and pressing it onto paper.

Expressionism an art style (1905–1920s) that was about feelings and emotions, often shown through distorted shapes or colours

grimace a twisted expression on a person's face, often showing disgust, pain or strange amusement

illuminated manuscript a book or other text that includes decorative initials, borders and miniature illustrations

illustrate to create pictures for a book or other piece of writing

lens a piece of glass with curved sides, used in cameras to focus light

monogram two or more letters, usually initials, woven into a design as a type of signature or logo

mural a painting made directly onto a wall. When a mural is painted on fresh, wet plaster, this is called a fresco.

ochre an earthy, brownish-yellow pigment

oil paint a thick type of paint made by mixing powdered pigments with an oil such as linseed

palette a board that an artist mixes paint on

pastel a type of soft crayon

pigment the natural colouring found in minerals, plants and animal matter. Nowadays, synthetic pigments are often used to make paints.

Pop Art an art style (mid-1950s–1960s) that celebrated the bold, bright images of advertising, cartoon strips and popular culture

portrait an artwork that shows an image of a particular person

Renaissance a period in European history (1300s–1500s) when there were great developments in art and culture, based on the ideas of Ancient Greece and Rome

sculpt to create a 3D artwork, or sculpture, using methods such as carving, modelling or casting. Someone who sculpts is called a sculptor.

silkscreen printing making a print by dragging ink over a stencil marked onto a silk screen. The ink goes through tiny holes in the silk that aren't covered by the stencil.

silverpoint drawing with a silver-pointed instrument onto a specially treated surface, creating a fine-lined design

sketch a rough or unfinished drawing or painting, often done in preparation for a finished work

studio an artist's workplace

Surrealism an art style (1924–1940s) that explored the world of dreams, the imagination and the 'non-thinking' mind. Surrealist works often show familiar things, but in unexpected ways.

texture the feel of a surface, such as rough hair or smooth glass

woodcut print a print made by carving an image into a block of wood, spreading ink over it then pressing it onto paper

Index